KIDS' SONGS for UKULELE

ISBN 978-1-4803-8285-5

HAL•LEONARD®
CORPORATION

7777 W. BLUEMOUND RD. P.O. BOX 13819 MILWAUKEE, WI 53213

Visit Hal Leonard Online at
www.halleonard.com

CONTENTS

Animal Fair

American Folksong

First note

Chorus
Lightly, in 2

I went to the an - i - mal fair, _____ the birds and beasts were

there. _____ The big ba - boon, by the light of the moon, was

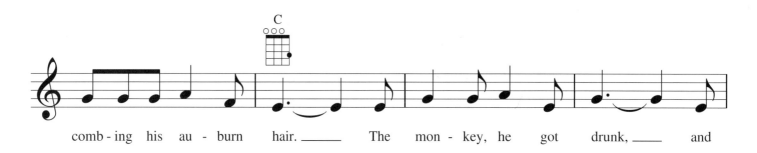

comb - ing his au - burn hair. _____ The mon - key, he got drunk, _____ and

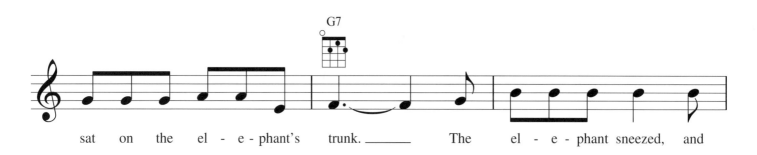

sat on the el - e - phant's trunk. _____ The el - e - phant sneezed, and

fell on his knees, and what be - came of the monk, the monk, the monk, the monk?

"C" Is for Cookie

Words and Music by Joe Raposo

Verse
Moderately

1., 2., 4. C is for cook-ie, that's good e-nough for me! C is for cook-ie, that's
3. (Spoken:) A round cookie with one bite out of it looks like a C. A round doughnut with one

good e-nough for me! C is for cook-ie, that's good e-nough for me! Oh,
bite out of it looks like a C, *but it is not as good as a cookie.* *Oh, and the*

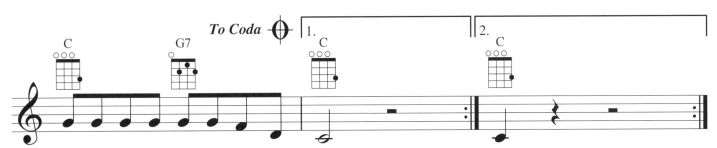

To Coda

cook-ie, cook-ie, cook-ie starts with C. C. (Spoken:) Hey, you know what?
moon sometimes looks like a C,

3.
D.C. al Coda   **Coda**

but you can't eat that. So   C. Yeah! Cook-ie, cook-ie, cook-ie starts with

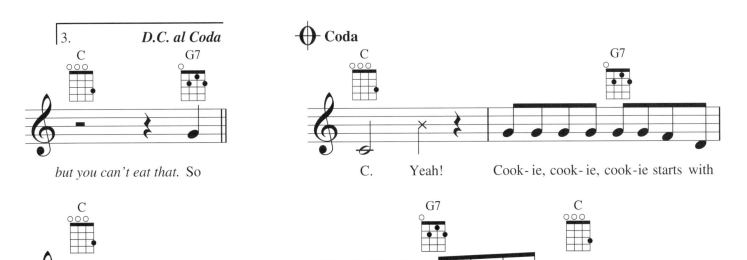

C. Oh boy! Cook-ie, cook-ie, cook-ie starts with C.

The Candy Man

from WILLY WONKA AND THE CHOCOLATE FACTORY

Words and Music by Leslie Bricusse and Anthony Newley

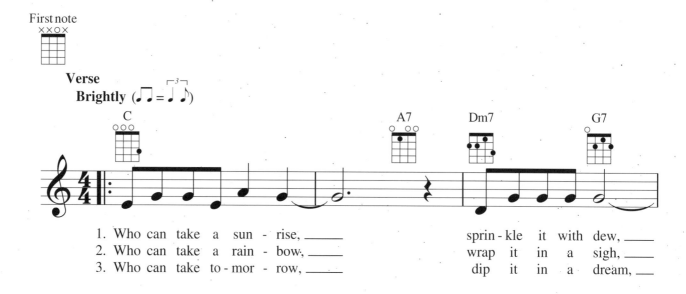

1. Who can take a sun - rise, _____ sprin - kle it with dew, _____
2. Who can take a rain - bow, _____ wrap it in a sigh, _____
3. Who can take to - mor - row, _____ dip it in a dream, _____

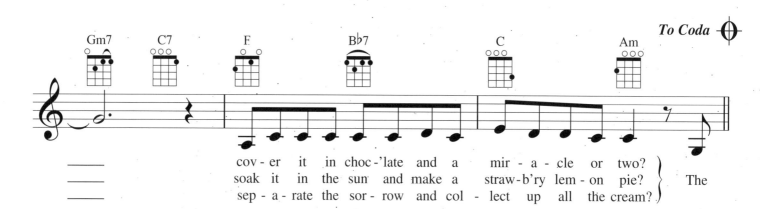

_____ cov - er it in choc - 'late and a mir - a - cle or two?
_____ soak it in the sun and make a straw - b'ry lem - on pie? } The
_____ sep - a - rate the sor - row and col - lect up all the cream?

Chorus

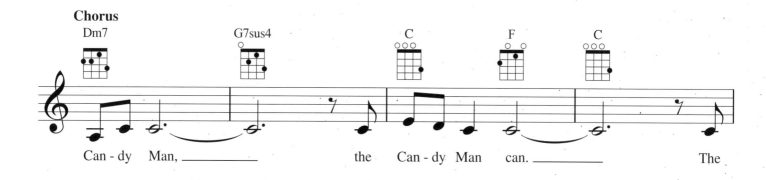

Can - dy Man, _____ the Can - dy Man can. _____ The

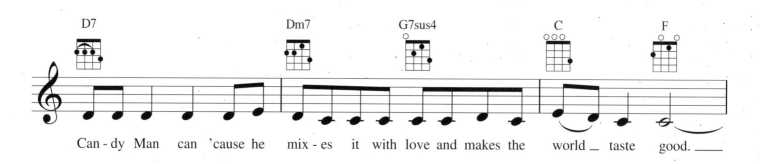

Can - dy Man can 'cause he mix - es it with love and makes the world _ taste good. _____

Ding-Dong! The Witch Is Dead

from THE WIZARD OF OZ
Lyric by E.Y. "Yip" Harburg
Music by Harold Arlen

Bridge

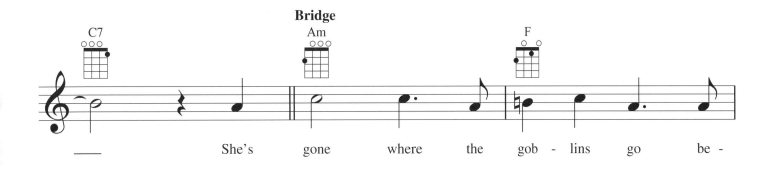

_____ She's gone where the gob - lins go be -

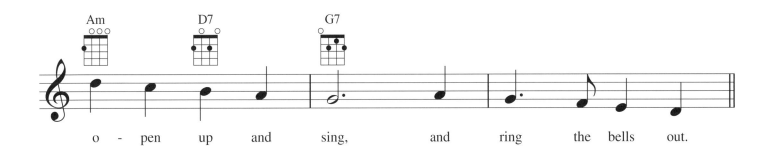

low, be - low, be - low, yo - ho, let's

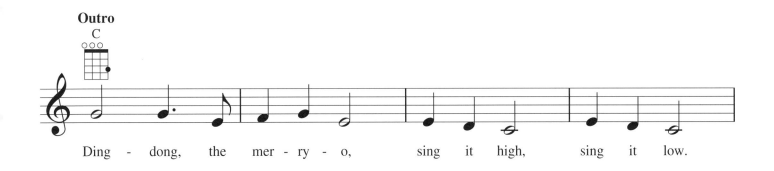

o - pen up and sing, and ring the bells out.

Outro

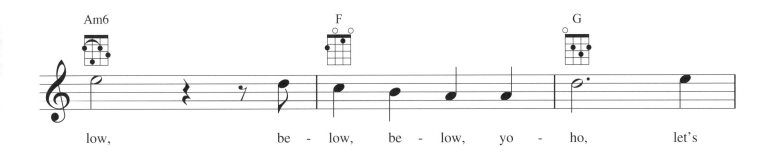

Ding - dong, the mer - ry - o, sing it high, sing it low.

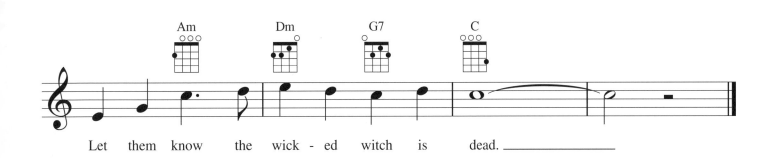

Let them know the wick - ed witch is dead. _____

Do-Re-Mi

from THE SOUND OF MUSIC
Lyrics by Oscar Hammerstein II
Music by Richard Rodgers

Happy Birthday to You

Words and Music by Mildred J. Hill and Patty S. Hill

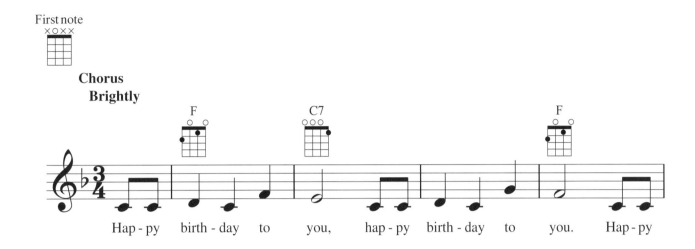

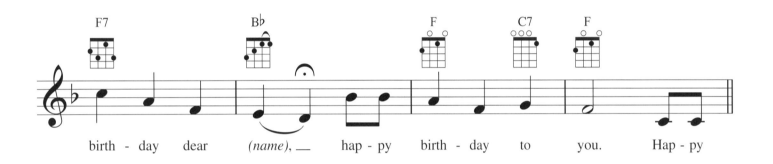

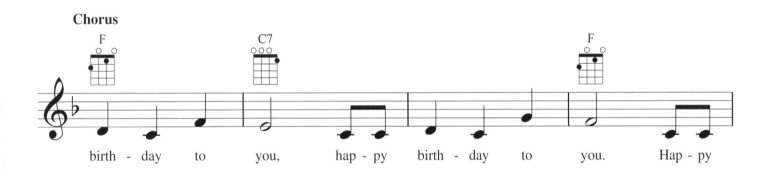

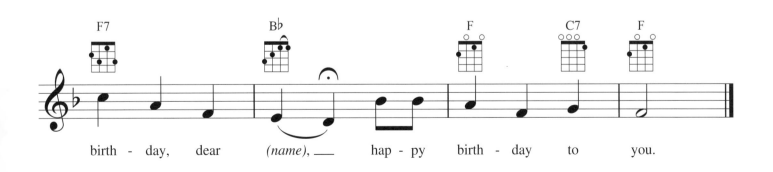

Elmo's Song

Words and Music by Tony Geiss

This is the song, la la la la, El - mo's song.

La la la la, la la la la,

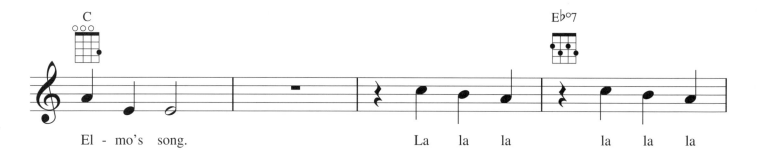

El - mo's song. La la la la la la

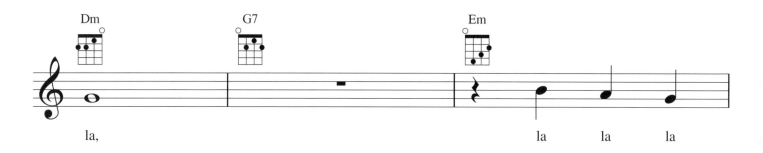

la, la la la la

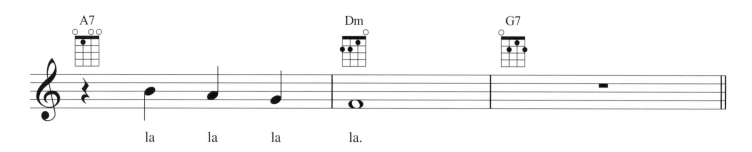

la la la la.

Chorus

He loves to sing, la la la la, El - mo's song.

La la la la, la la la la,

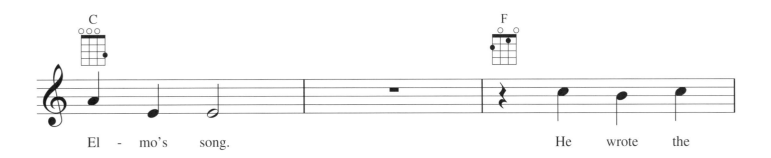

El - mo's song. He wrote the

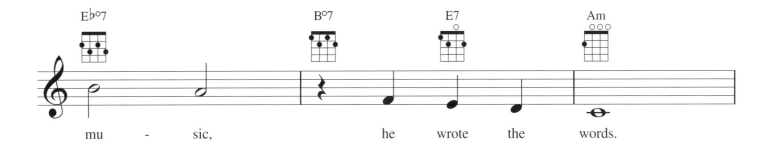

mu - sic, he wrote the words.

That's El - mo's song.

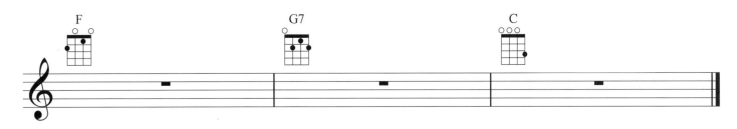

For He's a Jolly Good Fellow

Traditional

First note

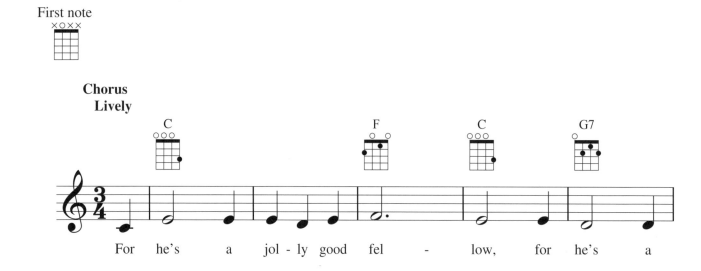

Chorus
Lively

For he's a jol - ly good fel - low, for he's a

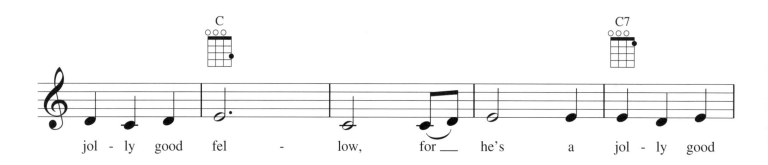

jol - ly good fel - low, for __ he's a jol - ly good

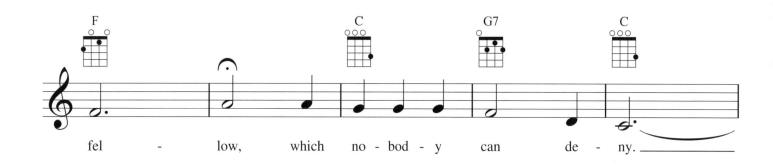

fel - low, which no - bod - y can de - ny. _____

Bridge

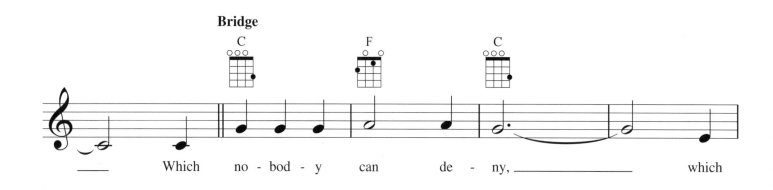

___ Which no - bod - y can de - ny, _____ which

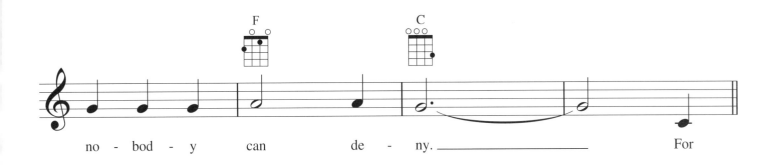

no - bod - y can de - ny. _____ For

Chorus

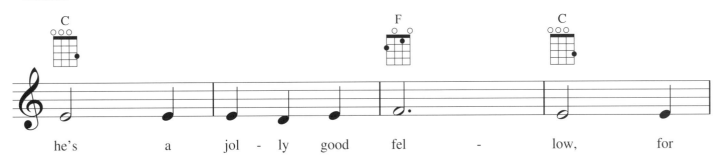

he's a jol - ly good fel - low, for

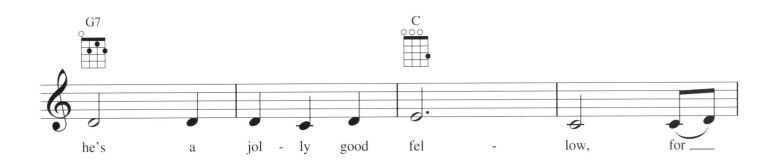

he's a jol - ly good fel - low, for ____

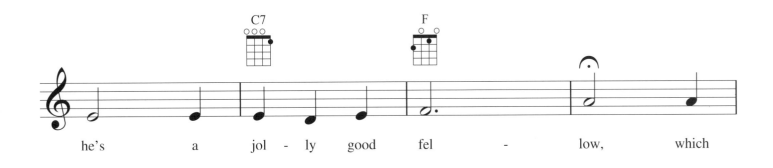

he's a jol - ly good fel - low, which

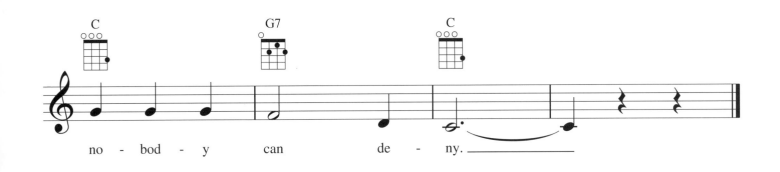

no - bod - y can de - ny. _____

Getting to Know You

from THE KING AND I

Lyrics by Oscar Hammerstein II
Music by Richard Rodgers

Heart and Soul

from the Paramount Short Subject A SONG IS BORN
Words by Frank Loesser
Music by Hoagy Carmichael

First note

Chorus
Moderately

1.	Heart	and	soul,		I	fell	in	love	with	you.
2.	Heart	and	soul,		I	begged	to	be	a -	dored.
(3.)	now	I	see		what	one	em -	brace	can	do.

Heart	and	soul,		the	way	a	fool	would	do,
Lost	con -	trol		and	tum -	bled	o -	ver -	board,
Look	at	me,		it's	got	me	lov -	ing	you

To Coda

mad	-	ly		be -	cause	you	held	me
glad	-	ly		that	mag -	ic	night	we
mad	-	ly,		that	lit -	tle	kiss	you

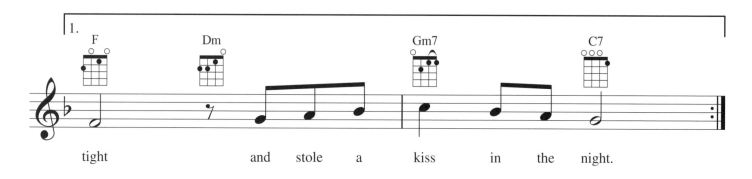

1.

| tight | | and | stole | a | kiss | in | the | night. |

kissed   there   in   the   moon - mist.

Bridge

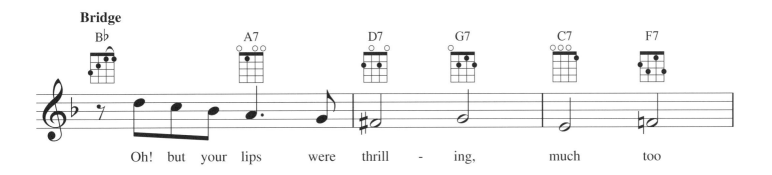

Oh! but your lips   were   thrill - ing,   much   too

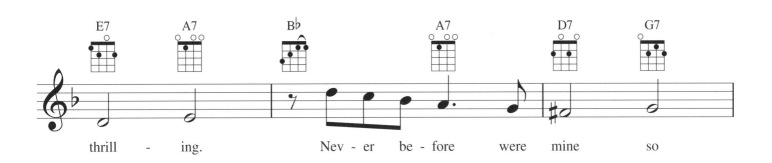

thrill - ing.   Nev - er be - fore   were   mine   so

D.C. al Coda   ⊕ **Coda**

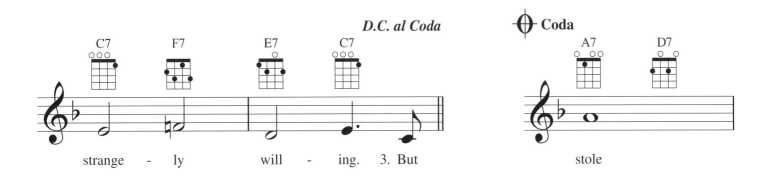

strange - ly   will - ing.   3. But   stole

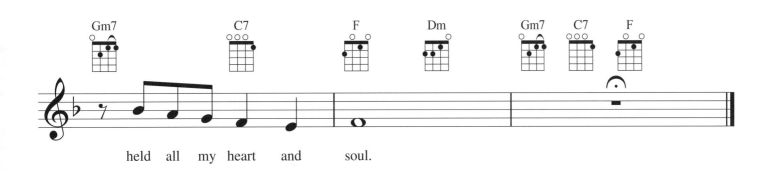

held   all   my   heart   and   soul.

Heigh-Ho

The Dwarfs' Marching Song from Walt Disney's SNOW WHITE AND THE SEVEN DWARFS
Words by Larry Morey
Music by Frank Churchill

I Whistle a Happy Tune

from THE KING AND I
Lyrics by Oscar Hammerstein II
Music by Richard Rodgers

Bridge

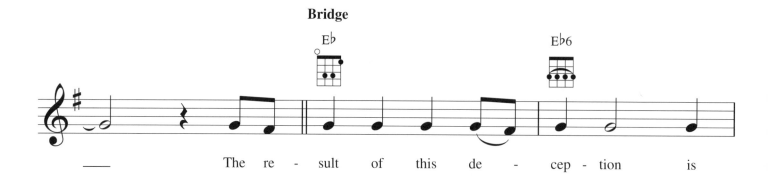

The re - sult of this de - cep - tion is

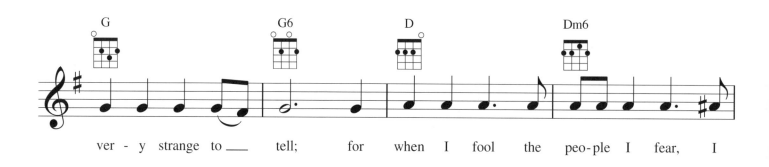

ver - y strange to ___ tell; for when I fool the peo-ple I fear, I

Chorus

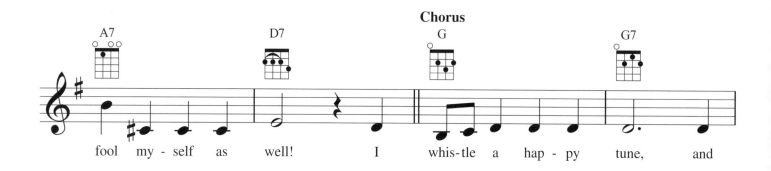

fool my - self as well! I whis-tle a hap - py tune, and

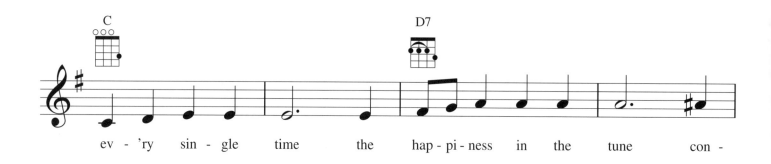

ev - 'ry sin - gle time the hap - pi - ness in the tune con -

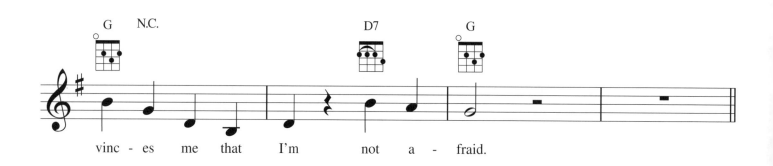

vinc - es me that I'm not a - fraid.

Outro

Make be - lieve you're brave and the trick will take you far.

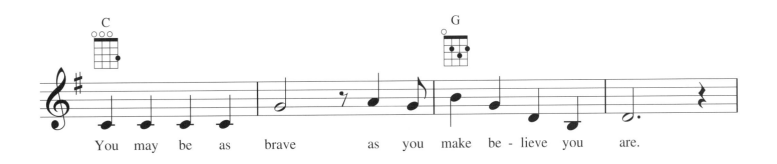

You may be as brave as you make be - lieve you are.

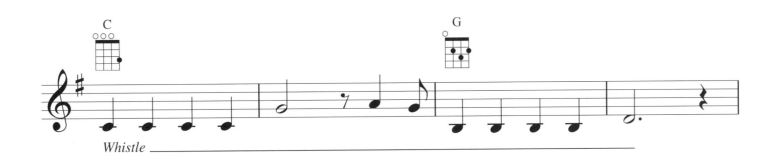

Whistle _____

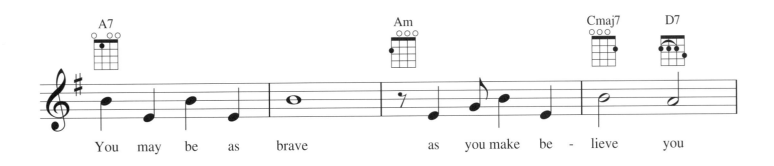

You may be as brave as you make be - lieve you

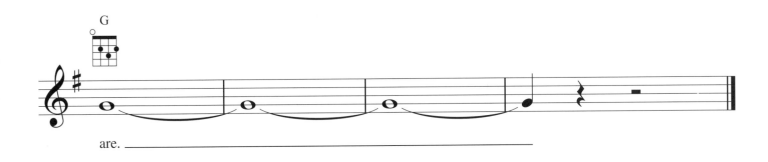

are. _____

Hi-Lili, Hi-Lo

Words by Helen Deutsch
Music by Bronislau Kaper

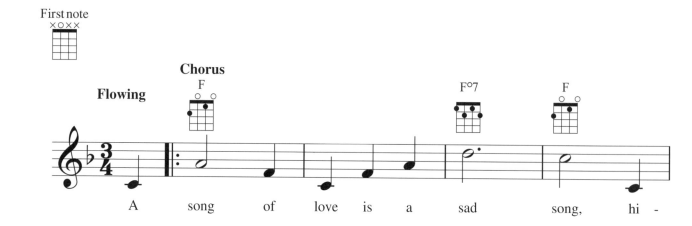

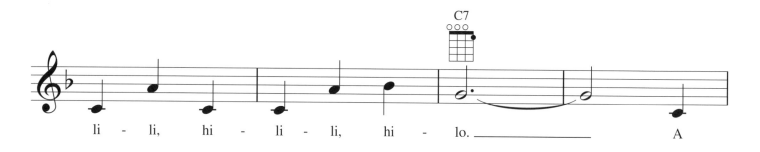

A song of love is a sad song, hi-

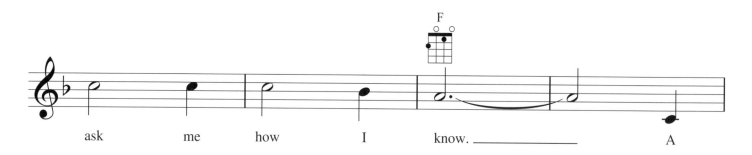

li-li, hi-li-li, hi-lo. _____ A

song of love is a song of woe, don't

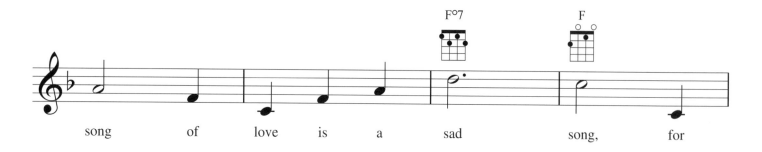

ask me how I know. _____ A

song of love is a sad song, for

The Hokey Pokey

Words and Music by Charles P. Macak, Tafft Baker and Larry LaPrise

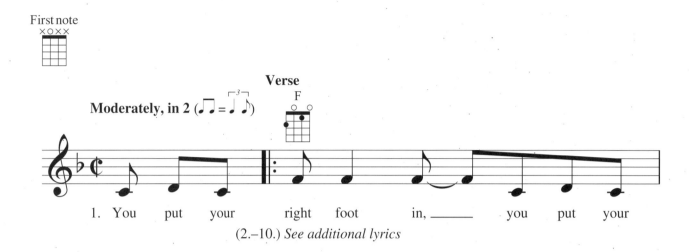

First note

Verse

Moderately, in 2

F

1. You put your right foot in, _____ you put your

(2.–10.) See additional lyrics

right foot out. _____ You put your right foot in, _____ and you

C7

shake it all a-bout. You do the Hok-ey Pok-ey, and you

turn your-self a-round. That's what it's all a-

Chorus

bout.　　　　You　do　the　Hok　-　ey

Pok　-　ey.　　　　You　do　the　Hok　-　ey

Pok　-　ey.　　　　You　do　the　Hok　-　ey

Pok　-　ey.　　　　That's　what　it's　all　a -

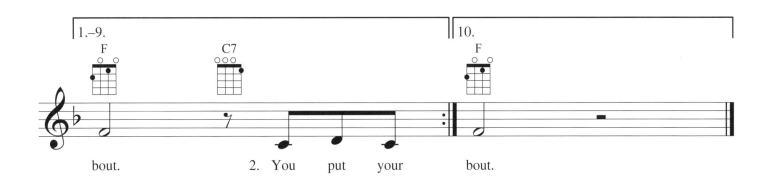

bout.　　　2. You　put　your　bout.

Additional Lyrics

2nd time: left foot
3rd time: right arm
4th time: left arm
5th time: right elbow
6th time: left elbow

7th time: head
8th time: right hip
9th time: left hip
10th time: whole self

Home on the Range

Lyrics by Dr. Brewster Higley
Music by Dan Kelly

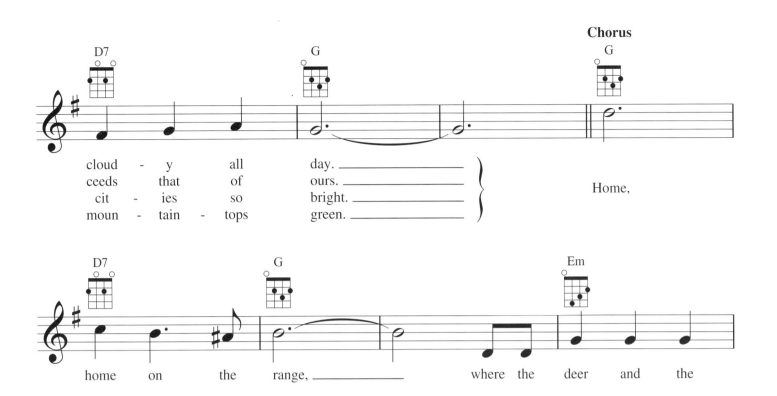

cloud - y all day. _____
ceeds that of ours. _____
cit - ies so bright. _____
moun - tain - tops green. _____

Home,

Chorus

home on the range, _____ where the deer and the

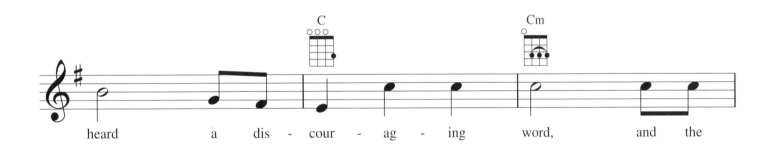

an - te - lope play. _____ Where sel - dom is

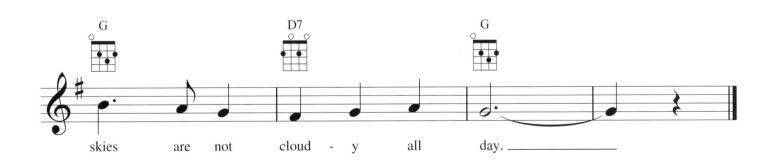

heard a dis - cour - ag - ing word, and the

skies are not cloud - y all day. _____

How Much Is That Doggie in the Window

Words and Music by Bob Merrill

First note

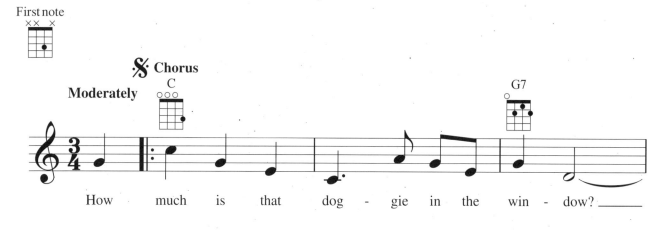

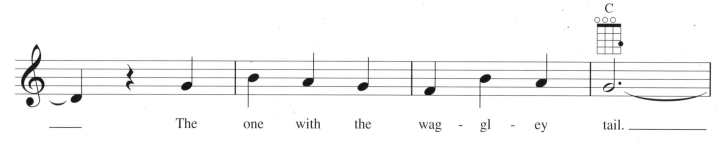

How much is that dog - gie in the win - dow? _____

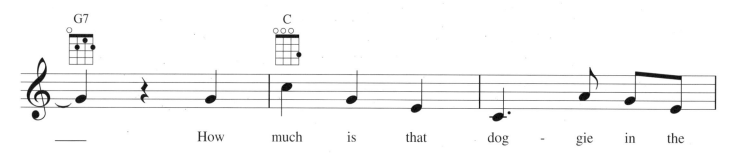

_____ The one with the wag - gl - ey tail. _____

_____ How much is that dog - gie in the

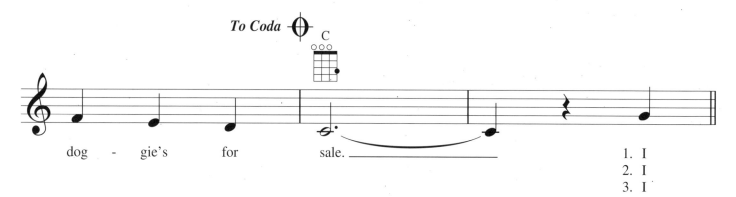

win - dow? _____ I do hope that

dog - gie's for sale. _____

1. I
2. I
3. I

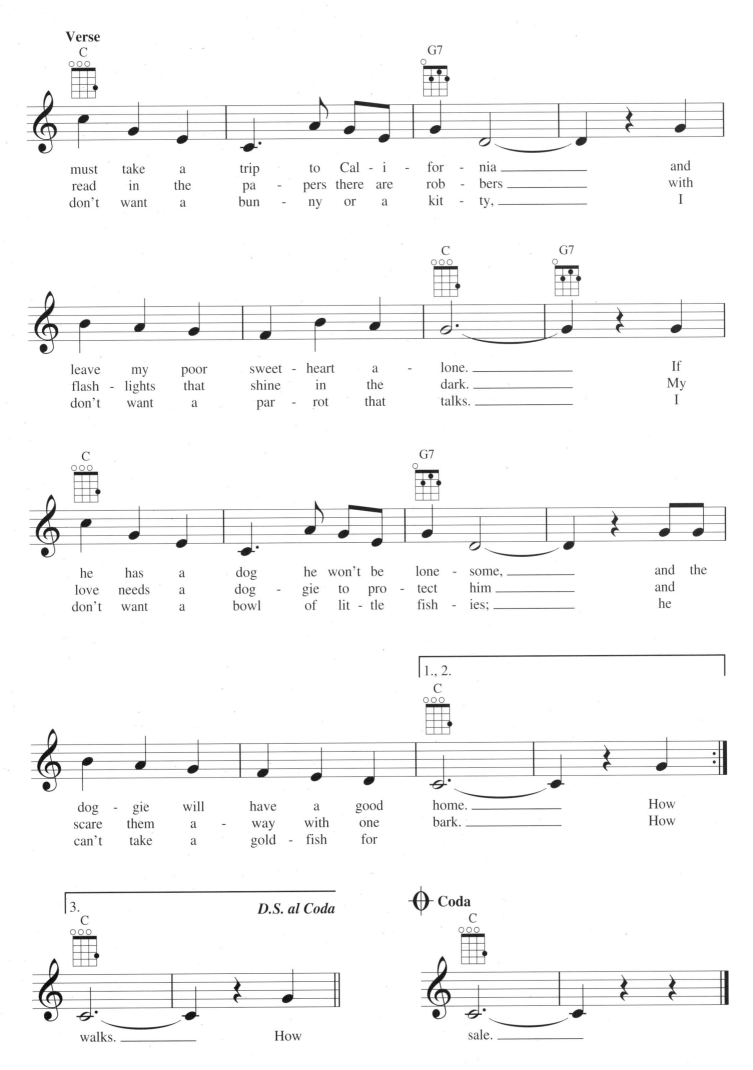

Verse

C   G7

must take a trip to Cal - i - for - nia _____ and
read in the pa - pers there are rob - bers _____ with
don't want a bun - ny or a kit - ty, _____ I

C   G7

leave my poor sweet - heart a - lone. _____ If
flash - lights that shine in the dark. _____ My
don't want a par - rot that talks. _____ I

C   G7

he has a dog he won't be lone - some, _____ and the
love needs a dog - gie to pro - tect him _____ and
don't want a bowl of lit - tle fish - ies; _____ he

1., 2.

C

dog - gie will have a good home. _____ How
scare them a - way with one bark. _____ How
can't take a gold - fish one for

3.   *D.S. al Coda*

C

walks. _____ How

Coda

C

sale. _____

I've Been Working on the Railroad

American Folksong

It's a Small World

from Disneyland Resort® and Magic Kingdom® Park
Words and Music by Richard M. Sherman and Robert B. Sherman

The Marvelous Toy

Words and Music by Tom Paxton

Chorus

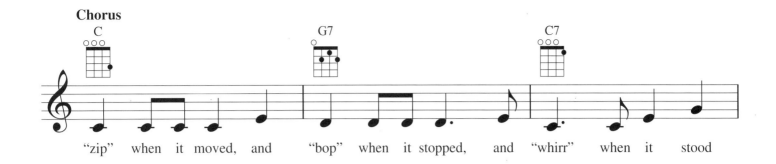

"zip" when it moved, and "bop" when it stopped, and "whirr" when it stood

still. I nev - er knew just what it was and I

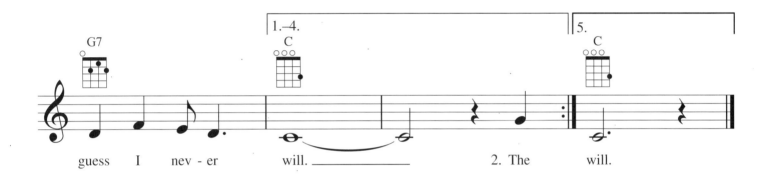

guess I nev - er will. _____ 2. The will.

Additional Lyrics

2. The first time that I picked it up, I had a big surprise,
   For right on its bottom were two big buttons that looked like big green eyes.
   I first pushed one and then the other, and then I twisted its lid,
   And when I set it down again, here is what it did:

3. It first marched left and then marched right and then marched under a chair,
   And when I looked where it had gone, it wasn't even there!
   I started to sob and my daddy laughed, for he knew that I would find
   When I turned around my marvelous toy, chugging from behind.

4. Well, the years have gone by too quickly, it seems,
   And I have my own little boy.
   And yesterday I gave to him my marvelous little toy.
   His eyes nearly popped right out of his head, and he gave a squeal of glee.
   Neither one of us knows just what it is, but he loves it, just like me.

Final Chorus: It still goes "zip" when it moves, and "bop" when it stops,
   And "whirr" when it stands still.
   I never knew just what it was
   And I guess I never will.

Mickey Mouse March

from Walt Disney's THE MICKEY MOUSE CLUB
Words and Music by Jimmie Dodd

If I Only Had a Brain

from THE WIZARD OF OZ

Lyric by E.Y. "Yip" Harburg
Music by Harold Arlen

First note

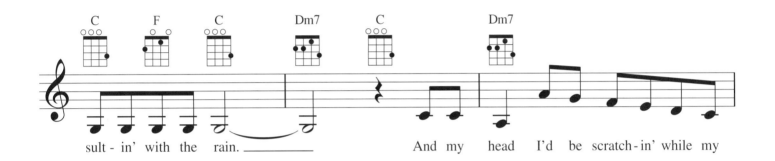

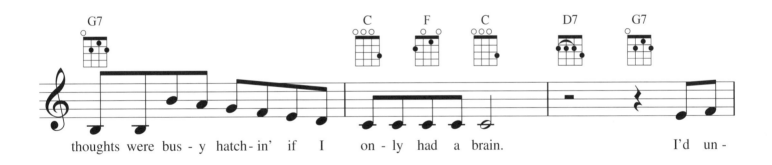

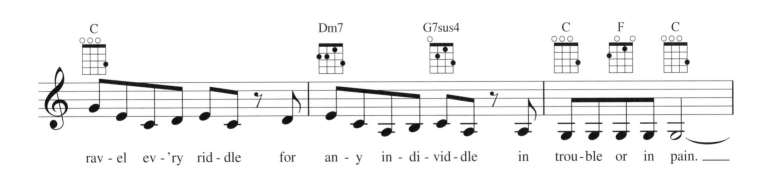

e - ven wor - thy erv you, if I on - ly had a brain.

Tin Woodman: 2. When a on - ly had the nerve.
Cowardly Lion: 3. Life is

Additional Lyrics

2. When a man's an empty kettle,
   He should be on his mettle, and yet I'm torn apart.
   Just because I'm presumin'
   That I could be kinda human if I only had a heart.
   I'd be tender, I'd be gentle
   And awful sentimental regarding love and art.
   I'd be friends with the sparrows
   And the boy that shoots the arrows, if I only had a heart.

Bridge: Picture me, a balcony, above a voice sings low,
   "Wherefore are thou, Romeo?"
   I hear a beat. How sweet!
   Just to register emotion,
   Jealousy, devotion, and really feel the part,
   I would stay young and chipper
   And I'd lock it with a zipper, if I only had a heart.

3. Life is sad, believe me, missy,
   When you're born to be a sissy, without the vim and verve.
   But I could change my habits,
   Never more be scared of rabbits if I only had the nerve.
   I'm afraid there's no denyin'
   I'm just a dandelion, a fate I don't deserve.
   But I could show my prowess,
   Be a lion, not a mow-ess, if I only had the nerve.

Bridge: Oh, I'd be in my stride, a king down to the core.
   Oh, I'd roar the way I never roared before,
   And then I'd rrrrwoof, and roar some more.
   I would show the dinosaurus
   Who's king around the forres', a king they better serve.
   Why, with my regal beezer,
   I could be another Caesar, if I only had the nerve.

My Favorite Things

from THE SOUND OF MUSIC

Lyrics by Oscar Hammerstein II
Music by Richard Rodgers

1. Rain - drops on ros - es and whisk - ers on
2. Cream - col - ored po - nies and crisp ap - ple

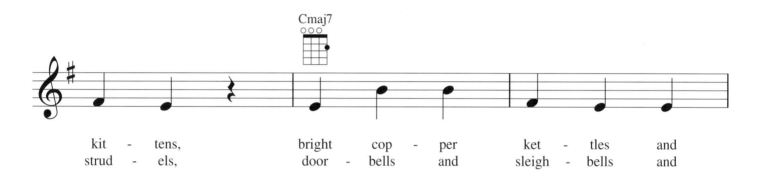

kit - tens, bright cop - per ket - tles and
strud - els, door - bells and sleigh - bells and

warm wool - en mit - tens, brown pa - per
schnitz - el with noo - dles, wild geese that

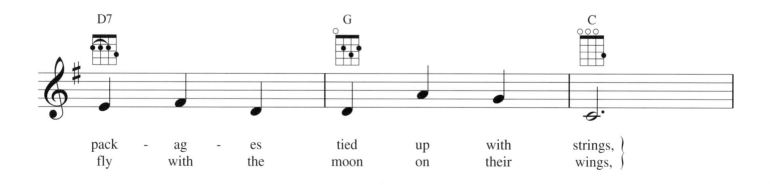

pack - ag - es tied up with strings,
fly with the moon on their wings,

these are a few of my fa - vor - ite

things.

fa - vor - ite things.

Verse

3. Girls in white dress - es with

blue sat - in sash - es, snow - flakes that

stay on my nose and eye - lash - es,

sil - ver white win - ters that melt in - to springs,

these   are   a   few   of   my   fa - vor - ite   things.

Outro

When   the   dog   bites,   when   the   bee   stings,

when   I'm   feel - ing   sad, _____   I

sim - ply   re - mem - ber   my   fa - vor - ite

things   and   then   I   don't   feel

so   bad. _____

Old MacDonald

Traditional Children's Song

First note

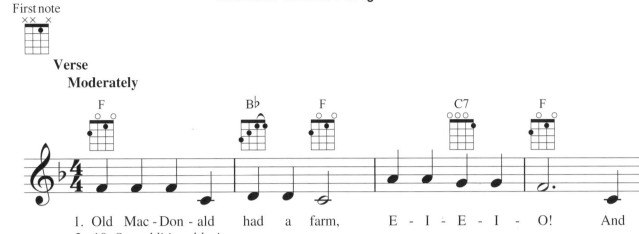

Verse
Moderately

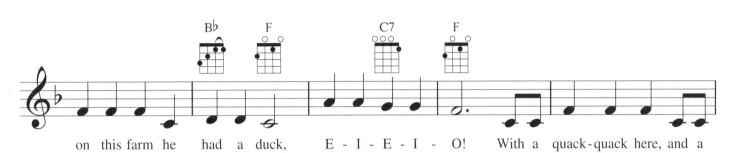

1. Old Mac - Don - ald   had a farm,   E - I - E - I - O!   And
2.–10. *See additional lyrics*

on this farm he   had a duck,   E - I - E - I - O!   With a quack-quack here, and a

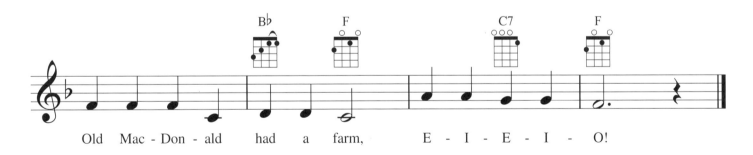

quack - quack there,   here a quack, there a quack,   ev - 'ry - where a quack, quack.

Old   Mac - Don - ald   had   a   farm,   E - I - E - I - O!

Additional Lyrics

2. Old MacDonald had a farm,
   E-I-E-I-O!
   And on his farm he had a chick,
   E-I-E-I-O!
   With a chick, chick here,
   And a chick, chick there,
   Here a chick, there a chick,
   Everywhere a chick, chick.
   Old MacDonald had a farm,
   E-I-E-I-O!

3. Cow – moo, moo
4. Dog – bow, bow
5. Pig – oink, oink
6. Rooster – cock-a-doodle, cock-a-doodle
7. Turkey – gobble, gobble
8. Cat – meow, meow
9. Horse – neigh, neigh
10. Donkey – hee-haw, hee-haw

Oh! Susanna

Words and Music by Stephen C. Foster

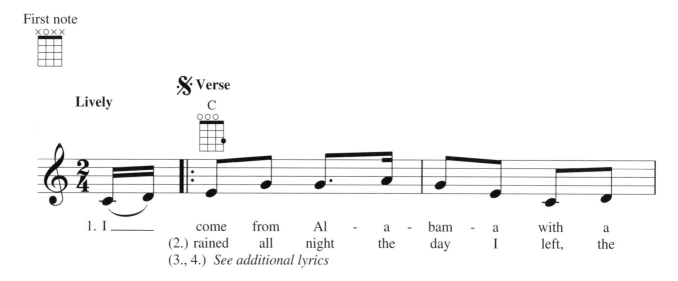

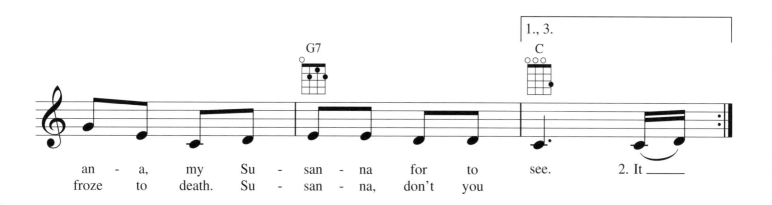

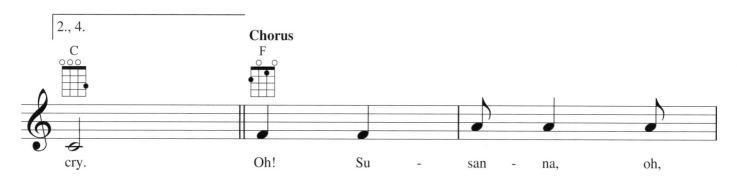

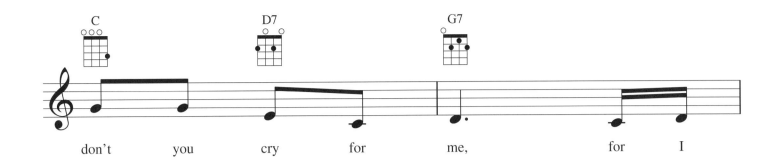

don't you cry for me, for I

come from Al - a - bam - a with a

To Coda ⊕

D.S. al Coda

⊕ **Coda**

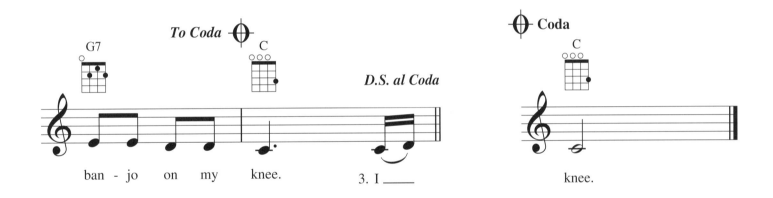

ban - jo on my knee.

3. I _____

knee.

Additional Lyrics

3. I had a dream the other night
   When everything was still.
   I thought I saw Susanna
   A-coming down the hill.

4. The buckwheat cake was in her mouth,
   The tear was in her eye,
   Say I, "I'm coming from the South.
   Susanna, don't you cry."

On Top of Spaghetti

Words and Music by Tom Glazer

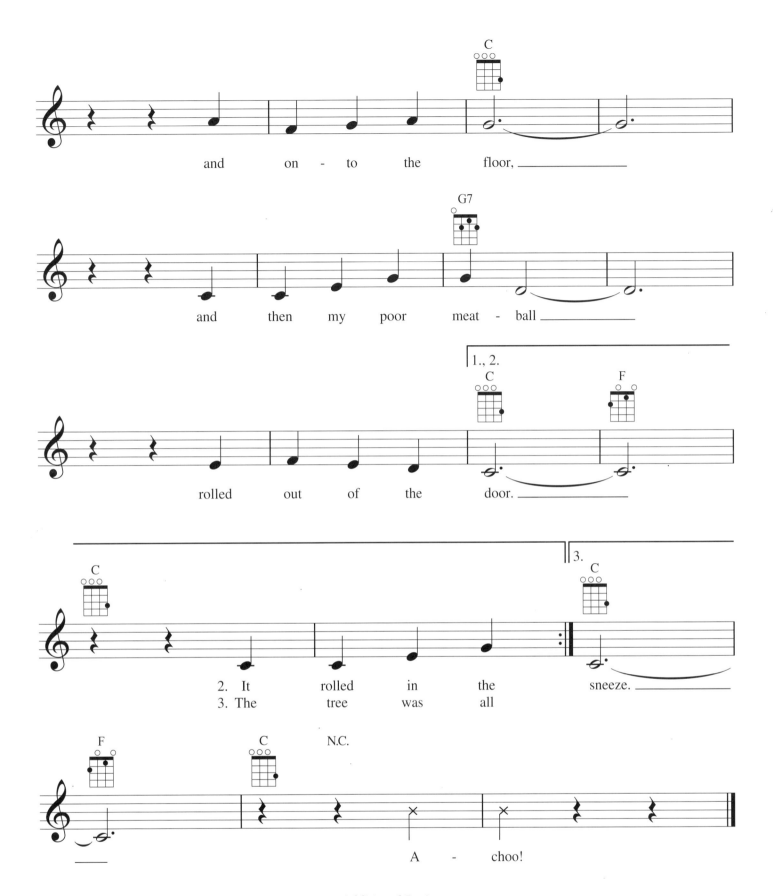

and   on - to   the   floor, _____

and   then   my   poor   meat - ball _____

1., 2.

rolled   out   of   the   door. _____

3.

2. It   rolled   in   the   sneeze. _____
3. The   tree   was   all

_____   A - choo!

Additional Lyrics

2. It rolled in the garden and under a bush,
   And then my poor meatball was nothing but mush.
   The mush was as tasty as tasty could be,
   And early next summer, it grew into a tree.

3. The tree was all covered with beautiful moss;
   It grew lovely meatballs and tomato sauce.
   So if you eat spaghetti all covered with cheese,
   Hold onto your meatballs and don't ever sneeze.

Over the Rainbow

from THE WIZARD OF OZ
Music by Harold Arlen
Lyric by E.Y. "Yip" Harburg

First note

Verse
Moderately, in 2

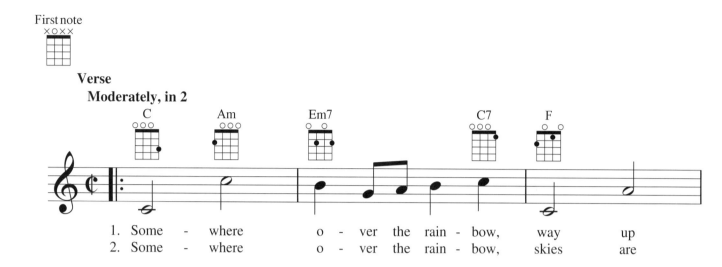

1. Some - where o - ver the rain - bow, way up
2. Some - where o - ver the rain - bow, skies are

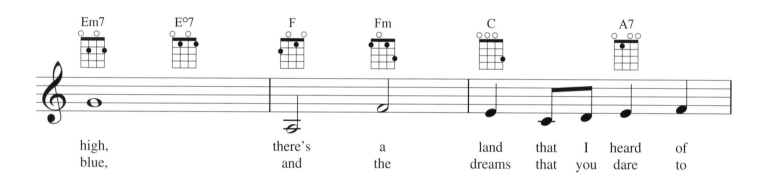

high, there's a land that I heard of
blue, and the dreams that you dare to

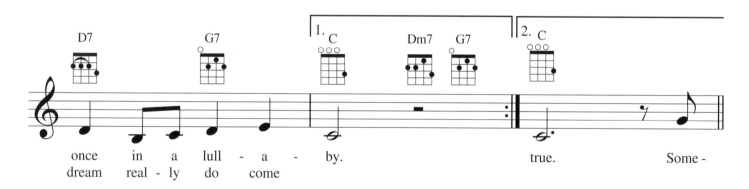

once in a lull - a - by. true. Some -
dream real - ly do come

Bridge

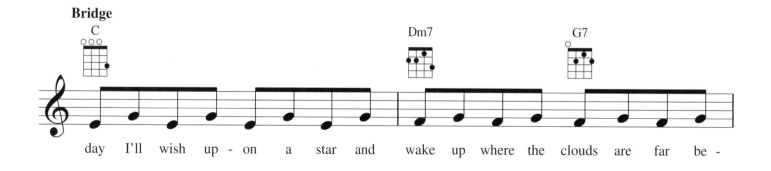

day I'll wish up - on a star and wake up where the clouds are far be -

hind me. _____ Where trou - bles melt like lem - on drops, a -

way, a - bove the chim - ney tops; that's where you'll find me.

Verse

3. Some - where o - ver the rain - bow, blue - birds

fly. Birds fly o - ver the rain - bow,

Outro

why, then, oh, why can't I? If hap - py lit - tle blue - birds fly be -

yond the rain - bow, why, oh, why can't I? _____

Peter Cottontail

Words and Music by Steve Nelson and Jack Rollins

1. Here comes Pe - ter Cot - ton - tail, hop - pin' down the
2. Here comes Pe - ter Cot - ton - tail, hop - pin' down the

bun - ny trail. ___ Hip - pi - ty hop - pin', Eas - ter's on its
bun - ny trail. ___ Look at him stop, and lis - ten to him

way. ___ Bring - in' ev - 'ry girl and boy
say, ___ "Try to do the things you should."

bas - kets full of Eas - ter joy, ___ things to make your
May - be if you're ex - tra good, ___ he'll roll lots of

Eas - ter bright and gay. ___ He's got
Eas - ter eggs your way. ___ You'll wake

Pop Goes the Weasel

Traditional

Puff the Magic Dragon

Words and Music by Lenny Lipton and Peter Yarrow

First note

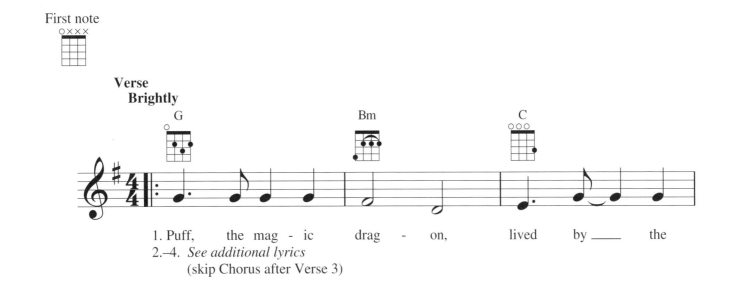

1. Puff, the mag - ic drag - on, lived by ____ the
2.–4. *See additional lyrics*
   (skip Chorus after Verse 3)

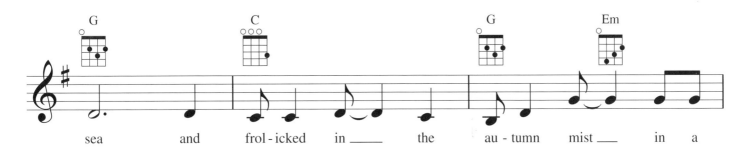

sea and frol - icked in ____ the au - tumn mist ____ in a

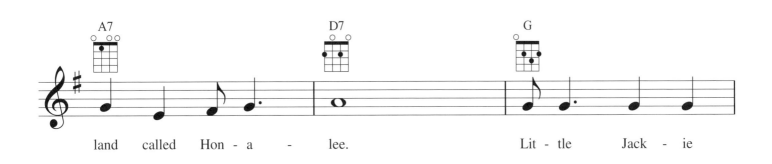

land called Hon - a - lee. Lit - tle Jack - ie

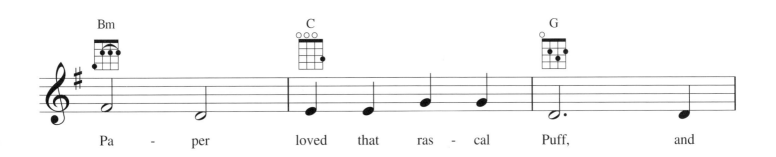

Pa - per loved that ras - cal Puff, and

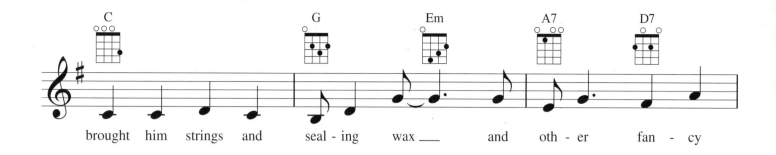

brought him strings and seal - ing wax ___ and oth - er fan - cy

Chorus

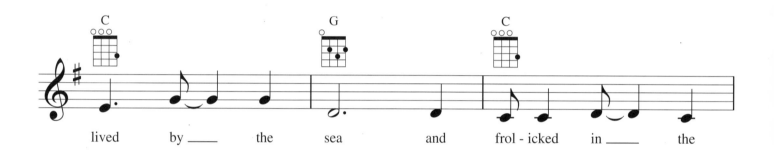

stuff. Oh, Puff, the mag - ic drag - on,

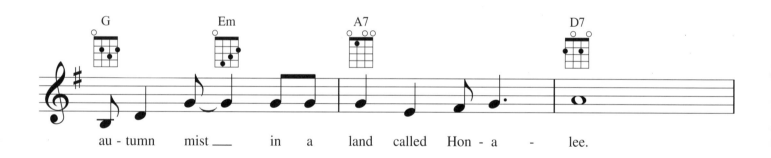

lived by ___ the sea and frol - icked in ___ the

au - tumn mist ___ in a land called Hon - a - lee.

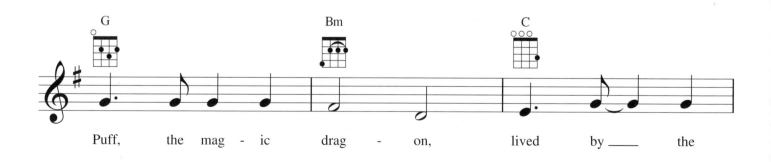

Puff, the mag - ic drag - on, lived by ___ the

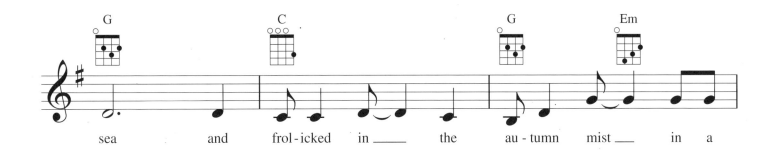

sea   and   frol - icked   in _____ the   au - tumn   mist __   in   a

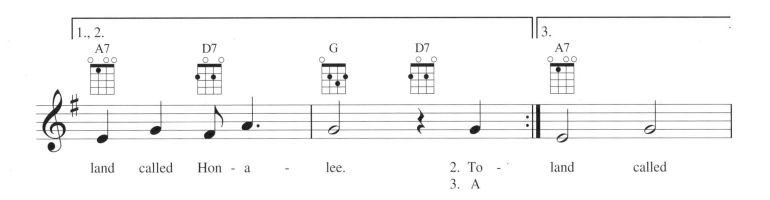

land   called   Hon - a - lee.   2. To -   land   called
                                                       3. A

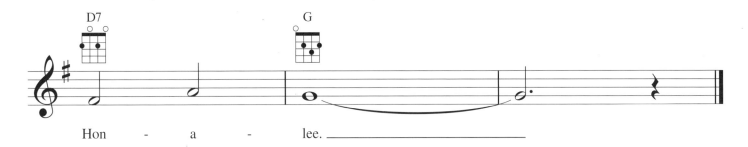

Hon - a - lee. _____

Additional Lyrics

2.   Together they would travel on a boat with billowed sail,
      And Jackie kept a lookout perched on Puff's gigantic tail.
      Noble kings and princes would bow whenever they came.
      Pirate ships would lower their flags when Puff roared out his name.

3.   A dragon lives forever, but not so little boys.
      Painted wings and giant rings make way for other toys.
      One gray night it happened; Jackie Paper came no more,
      And Puff, that mighty dragon, he ceased his fearless roar. *(To Verse 4)*

4.   His head was bent in sorrow, green tears fell like rain.
      Puff no longer went to play along the Cherry Lane.
      Without his lifelong friend, Puff could not be brave.
      So Puff, that mighty dragon, sadly slipped into his cave.

The Rainbow Connection

from THE MUPPET MOVIE

Words and Music by Paul Williams and Kenneth L. Ascher

First note

Verse
Flowing Waltz tempo

1. Why are there so man-y songs a-bout rain-bows and
2., 3. *See additional lyrics*

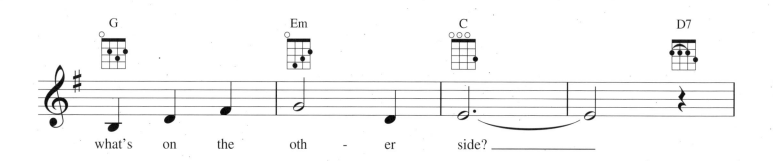

what's on the oth - er side? _____

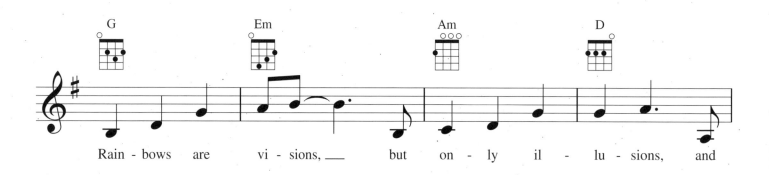

Rain - bows are vi - sions, ___ but on - ly il - lu - sions, and

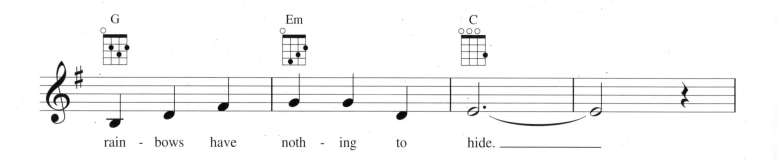

rain - bows have noth - ing to hide. _____

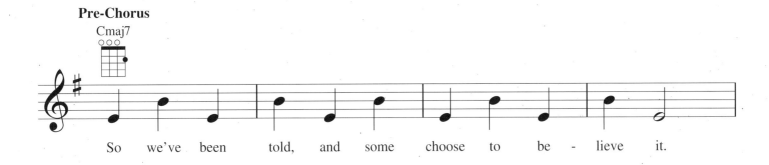

Pre-Chorus

Cmaj7

So we've been told, and some choose to be - lieve it.

F#m7

I know they're wrong; wait and see. _____

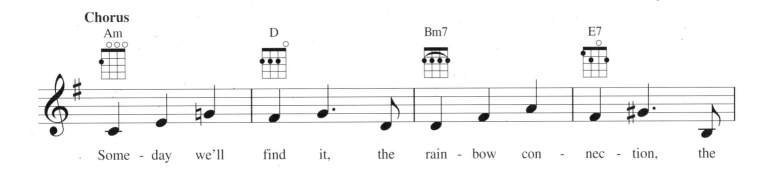

Chorus

Am   D   Bm7   E7

Some - day we'll find it, the rain - bow con - nec - tion, the

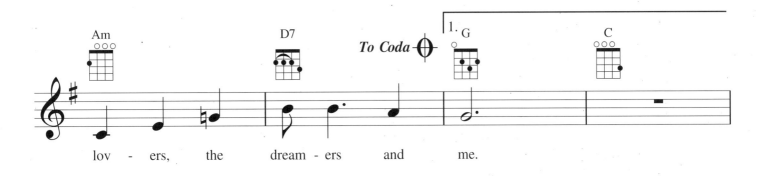

Am   D7   *To Coda* ⊕   1. G   C

lov - ers, the dream - ers and me.

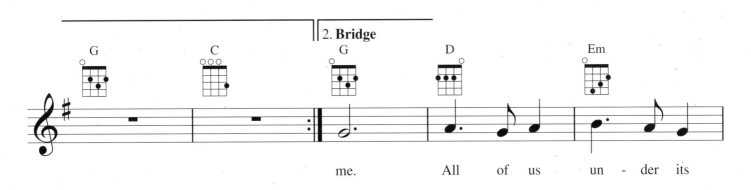

G   C   2. **Bridge**   G   D   Em

me.   All of us un - der its

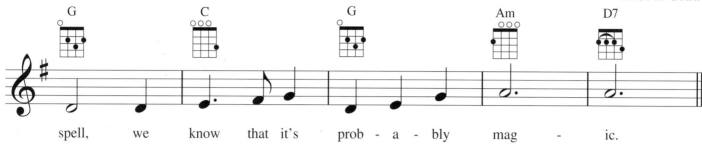

spell,   we   know   that   it's   prob - a - bly   mag   -   ic.

Coda
Outro

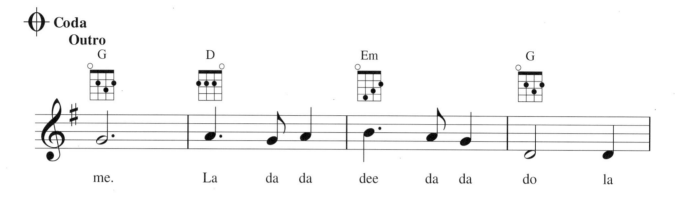

me.   La   da   da   dee   da   da   do   la

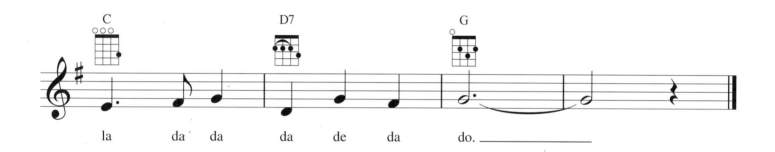

la   da   da   da   de   da   do. _____

Additional Lyrics

2. Who said that ev'ry wish would be heard and answered
   When wished on the morning star?
   Somebody thought of that and someone believed it;
   Look what it's done so far.
   What's so amazing that keeps us stargazing,
   And what do we think we might see?

3. Have you been half asleep and have you heard voices?
   I've heard them calling my name.
   Is this the sweet sound that calls the young sailors?
   The voice might be one and the same.
   I've heard it too many times to ignore it;
   It's something that I'm s'posed to be.

She'll Be Comin' 'Round the Mountain

Traditional

First note

Rhythmically

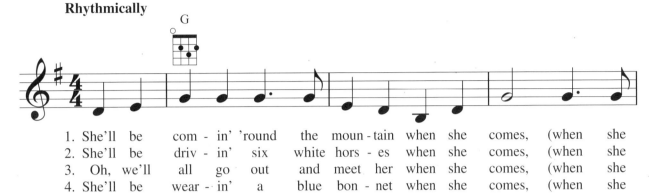

1. She'll be com-in' 'round the moun-tain when she comes, (when she
2. She'll be driv-in' six white hors-es when she comes, (when she
3. Oh, we'll all go out and meet her when she comes, (when she
4. She'll be wear-in' a blue bon-net when she comes, (when she

comes.) She'll be com-in' 'round the moun-tain when she comes, (when she
comes.) She'll be driv-in' six white hors-es when she comes, (when she
comes.) Oh, we'll all go out to meet her when she comes, (when she
comes.) She'll be wear-in' a blue bon-net when she comes, (when she

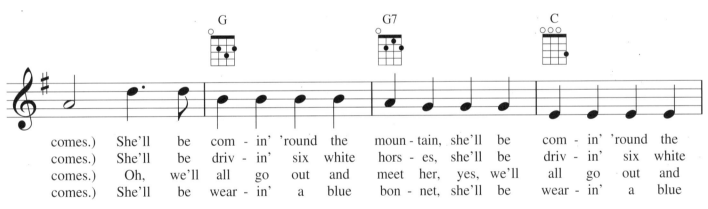

comes.) She'll be com-in' 'round the moun-tain, she'll be com-in' 'round the
comes.) She'll be driv-in' six white hors-es, she'll be driv-in' six white
comes.) Oh, we'll all go out and meet her, yes, we'll all go out and
comes.) She'll be wear-in' a blue bon-net, she'll be wear-in' a blue

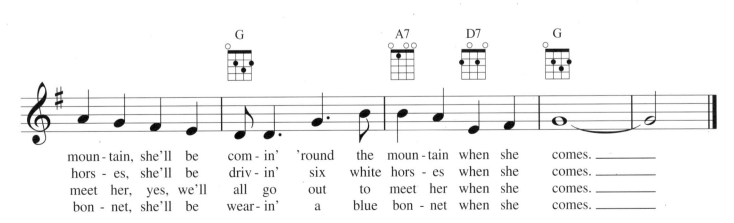

moun-tain, she'll be com-in' 'round the moun-tain when she comes. _____
hors-es, she'll be driv-in' six white hors-es when she comes. _____
meet her, yes, we'll all go out to meet her when she comes. _____
bon-net, she'll be wear-in' a blue bon-net when she comes. _____

Sesame Street Theme

Words by Bruce Hart, Jon Stone and Joe Raposo
Music by Joe Raposo

1., 3. Sun - ny day sweep - in' the clouds ___ a -
2. Come ___ and play! Ev - 'ry - thing's A - O -

way.   On _____ my   way   to where   the
K.   Friend - ly   neigh - bors there,   that's

air   is ___   sweet. _____ }   Can you   tell   me   how   to get,
where   we ___   meet. _____ }

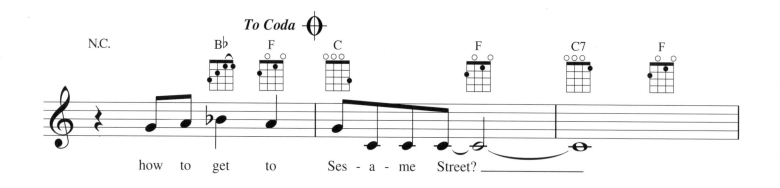

how   to get   to   Ses - a - me   Street? _____

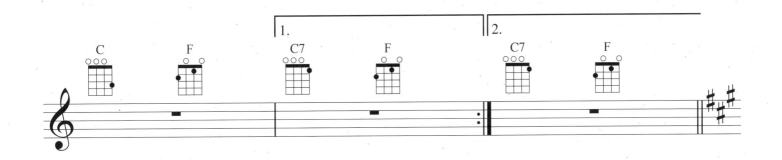

Bridge

It's a mag-ic car - pet ride. ___ Ev - 'ry door will o -

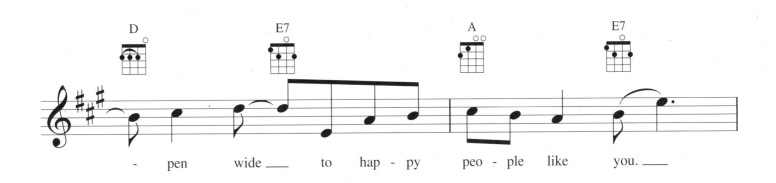

- pen wide ___ to hap - py peo - ple like you. ___

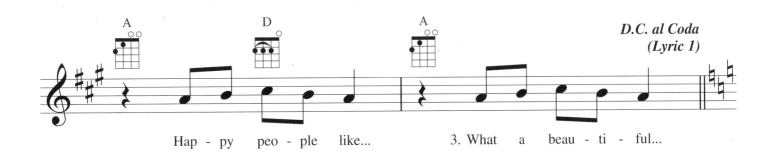

Hap - py peo - ple like... 3. What a beau - ti - ful...

D.C. al Coda
(Lyric 1)

Coda   *Repeat and fade*

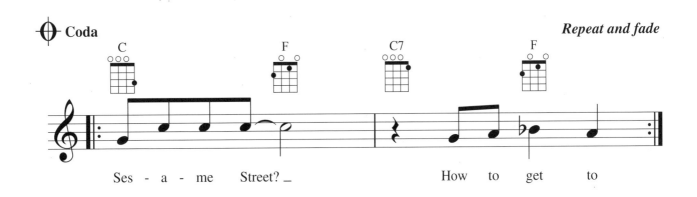

Ses - a - me Street? _ How to get to

Sing

from SESAME STREET
Words and Music by Joe Raposo

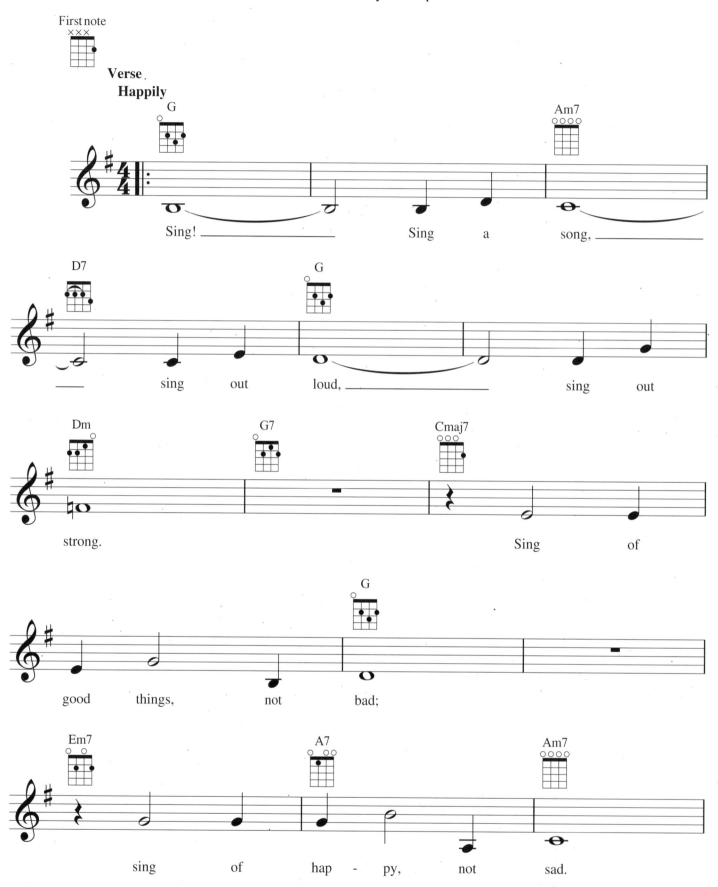

Splish Splash

Words and Music by Bobby Darin and Murray Kaufman

SpongeBob SquarePants Theme Song

from SPONGEBOB SQUAREPANTS

**Words and Music by Mark Harrison, Blaise Smith,
Steve Hillenburg and Derek Drymon**

Supercalifragilisticexpialidocious

from Walt Disney's MARY POPPINS

Words and Music by Richard M. Sherman and Robert B. Sherman

First note

Chorus
Brightly, in 2

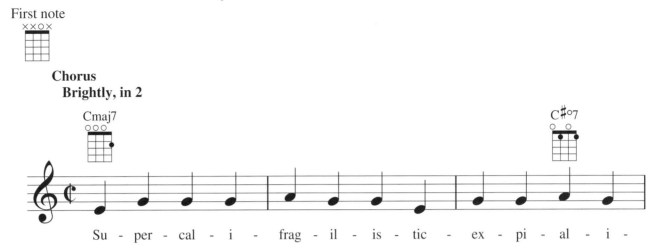

Su - per - cal - i - frag - il - is - tic - ex - pi - al - i -

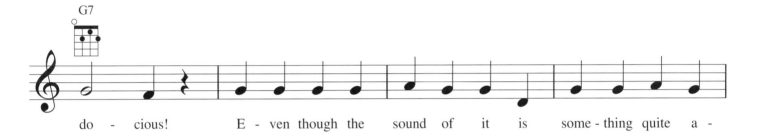

do - cious! E - ven though the sound of it is some - thing quite a -

tro - cious, if you say it loud e - nough, you'll

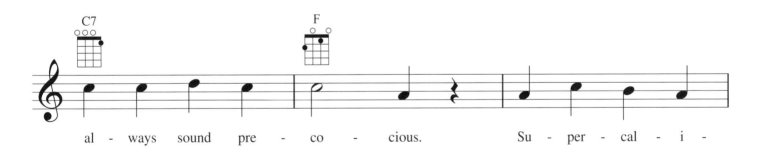

al - ways sound pre - co - cious. Su - per - cal - i -

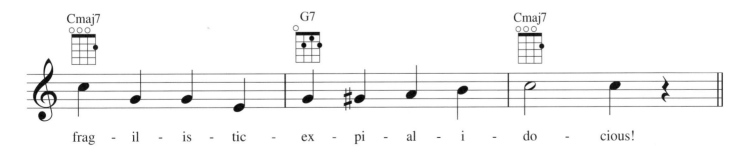

frag - il - is - tic - ex - pi - al - i - do - cious!

Take Me Out to the Ball Game

from TAKE ME OUT TO THE BALL GAME

Words by Jack Norworth
Music by Albert von Tilzer

First note

Brightly

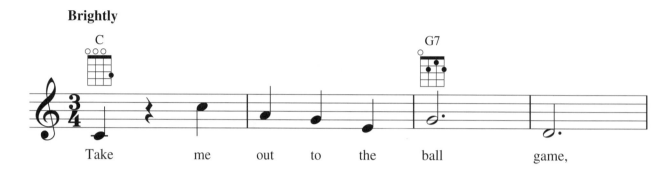

Take me out to the ball game,

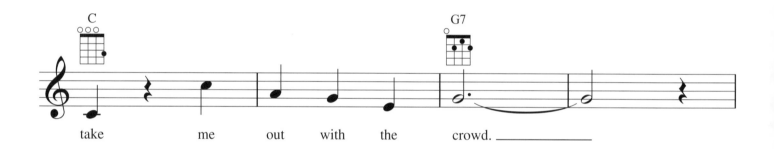

take me out with the crowd. _____

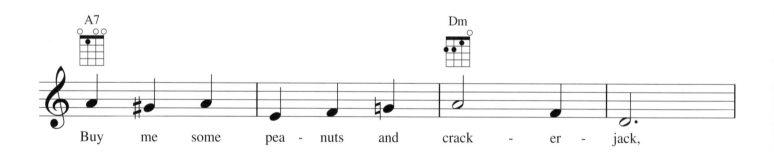

Buy me some pea - nuts and crack - er - jack,

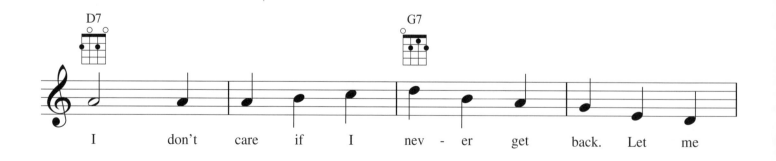

I don't care if I nev - er get back. Let me

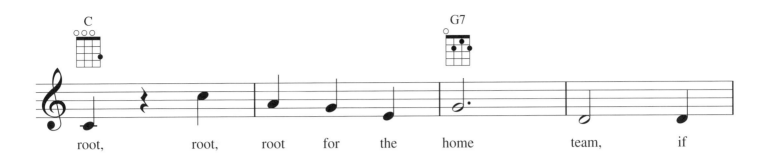

root,   root,   root   for   the   home   team,   if

they   don't   win   it's   a   shame. _____   For   it's

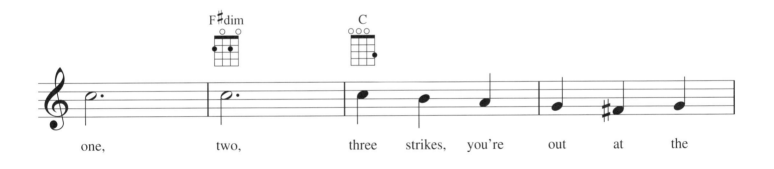

one,   two,   three   strikes,   you're   out   at   the

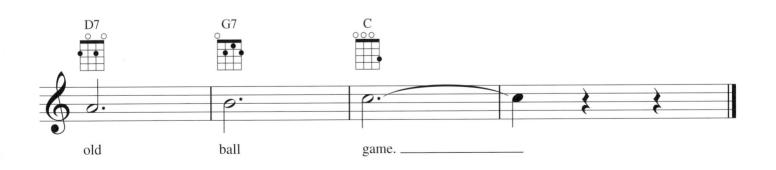

old   ball   game. _____

This Land Is Your Land

Words and Music by Woody Guthrie

Additional Lyrics

3. When the sun came shining, and I was strolling,
   And the wheat fields waving, and the dust clouds rolling,
   As the fog was lifting, a voice was chanting:
   This land was made for you and me.

4. As I went walking, I saw a sign there,
   And on the sign it said, "No Trespassing,"
   But on the other side it didn't say nothing;
   That side was made for you and me.

5. In the shadow of the steeple, I saw my people.
   By the relief office, I saw my people.
   As they stood there hungry, I stood there asking:
   Is this land made for you and me?

6. Nobody living can ever stop me
   As I go walking that freedom highway.
   Nobody living can ever make me turn back;
   This land was made for you and me.

Tomorrow

from the Musical Production ANNIE

Lyric by Martin Charnin
Music by Charles Strouse

First note

Chorus
Moderately slow

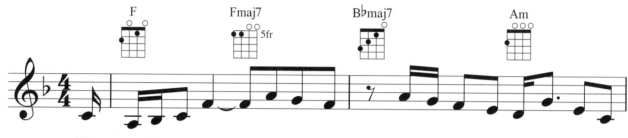

The sun-'ll come out ___ to-mor-row, bet your bot-tom dol-lar that to-

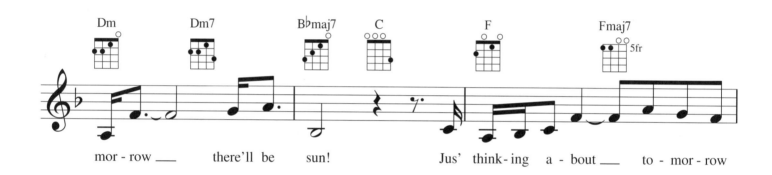

mor-row ___ there'll be sun! Jus' think-ing a-bout ___ to-mor-row

clears a-way the cob-webs and the sor-row ___ till there's

Bridge

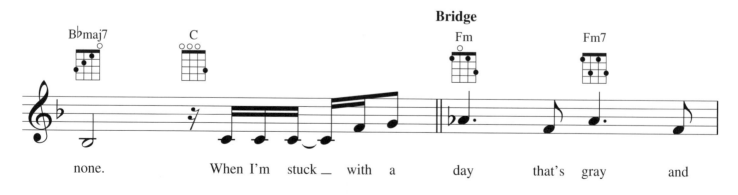

none. When I'm stuck ___ with a day that's gray and

lone - ly,   I   just   stick — out   my   chin   and   grin   and

Chorus

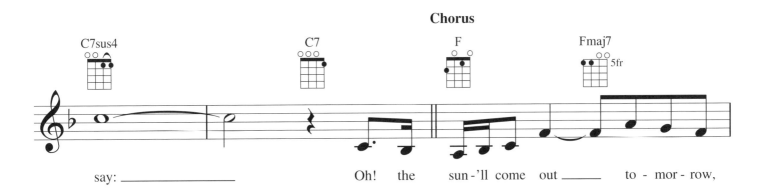

say: _____   Oh!   the   sun -'ll come out _____ to - mor - row,

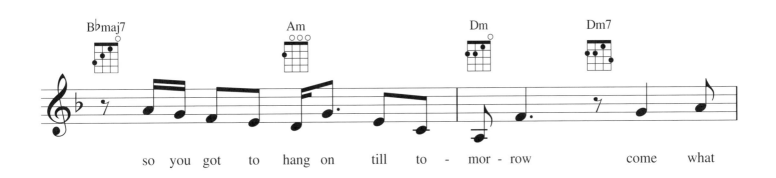

so   you   got   to   hang on   till   to - mor - row   come what

Outro

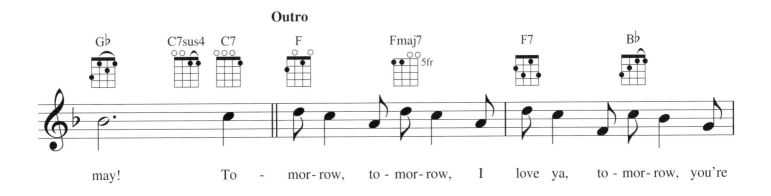

may!   To - mor - row,   to - mor - row,   I   love ya,   to - mor - row, you're

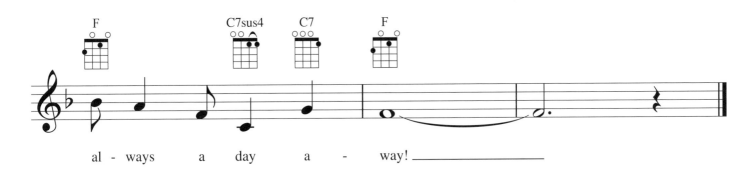

al - ways   a   day   a - way! _____

We're Off to See the Wizard

Lyric by E.Y. "Yip" Harburg
Music by Harold Arlen

When I Grow Too Old to Dream

Lyrics by Oscar Hammerstein II
Music by Sigmund Romberg

Yankee Doodle

Traditional

pud - ding.
saved. _
mil - lion.

Yan - kee Doo - dle, keep it up, Yan - kee Doo - dle dan - dy. Mind the mu - sic

and the step, and with the girls be hand - y. { 2.,4.,6. And   5. We   hand - y.

Additional Lyrics

4. And then the feathers on his hat,
   They looked so 'tarnel fine, ah!
   I wanted peskily to get
   To give to me Jemima.

5. We saw a little barrel, too,
   The heads were made of leather.
   They knocked on it with little clubs
   And called the folks together.

6. And there they'd fife away like fun,
   And play on cornstalk fiddles.
   And some had ribbons red as blood
   All bound around their middles.

Whistle While You Work

from Walt Disney's SNOW WHITE AND THE SEVEN DWARFS
Words by Larry Morey
Music by Frank Churchill

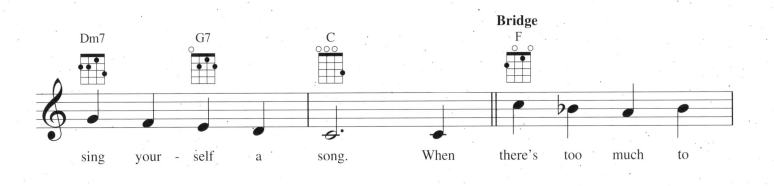

sing your - self a song. When there's too much to

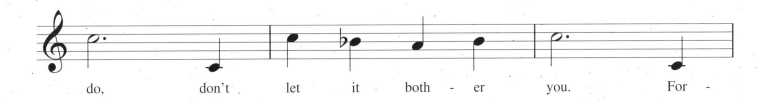

do, don't let it both - er you. For -

get your trou - ble, try to be just like the cheer - ful

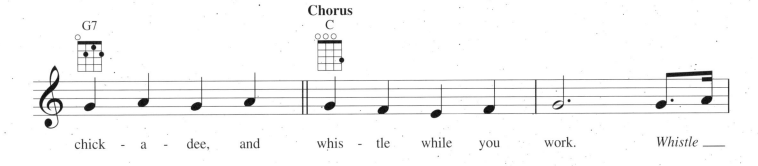

chick - a - dee, and whis - tle while you work. *Whistle* ___

Come on, get smart, tune

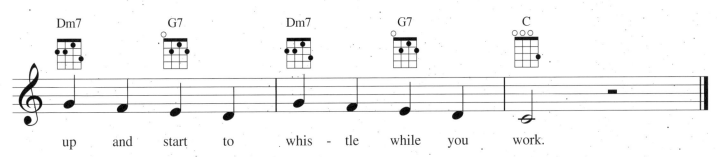

up and start to whis - tle while you work.

Yellow Submarine

from YELLOW SUBMARINE

Words and Music by John Lennon and Paul McCartney

Zip-A-Dee-Doo-Dah

from Walt Disney's SONG OF THE SOUTH
Words by Ray Gilbert
Music by Allie Wrubel

First note

Chorus
Merrily

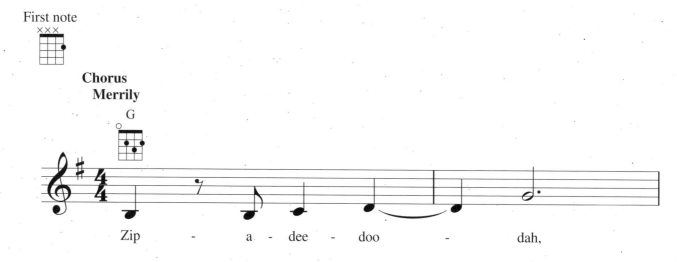

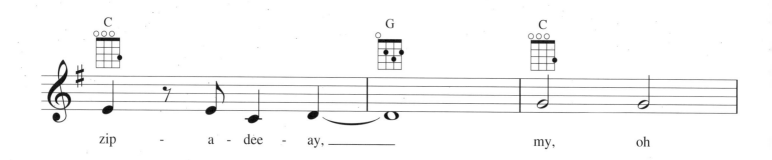

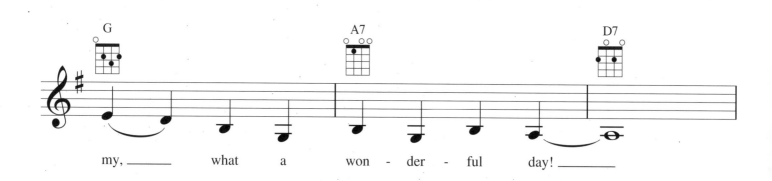

zip - a - dee - doo - dah,
Won - der - ful feel - ing,

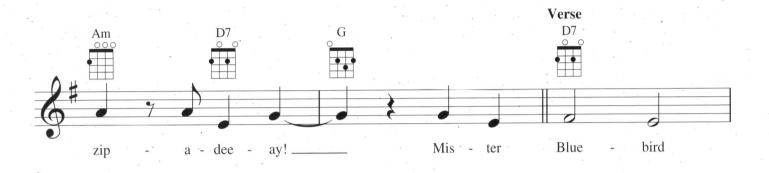

zip - a - dee - ay! _____ Mis - ter Blue - bird

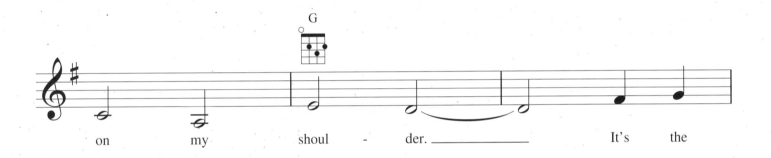

on my shoul - der. _____ It's the

truth, it's "act - ch'll," ev - 'ry - thing is

D.S. al Coda

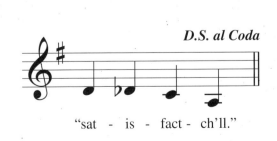

"sat - is - fact - ch'll."

Coda

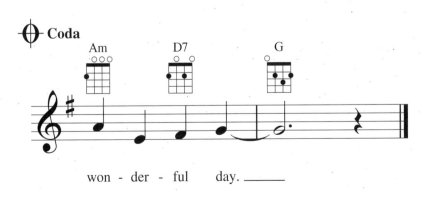

won - der - ful day. _____

HAL•LEONARD® UKULELE PLAY-ALONG

Now you can play your favorite songs on your uke with great-sounding backing tracks to help you sound like a bona fide pro! The audio also features playback tools so you can adjust the tempo without changing the pitch and loop challenging parts.

1. POP HITS
00701451 Book/CD Pack $15.99

3. HAWAIIAN FAVORITES
00701453 Book/Online Audio $14.99

4. CHILDREN'S SONGS
00701454 Book/Online Audio $14.99

5. CHRISTMAS SONGS
00701696 Book/CD Pack $12.99

6. LENNON & MCCARTNEY
00701723 Book/Online Audio $12.99

7. DISNEY FAVORITES
00701724 Book/Online Audio $14.99

8. CHART HITS
00701745 Book/CD Pack $15.99

9. THE SOUND OF MUSIC
00701784 Book/CD Pack $14.99

10. MOTOWN
00701964 Book/CD Pack $12.99

11. CHRISTMAS STRUMMING
00702458 Book/Online Audio $12.99

12. BLUEGRASS FAVORITES
00702584 Book/CD Pack $12.99

13. UKULELE SONGS
00702599 Book/CD Pack $12.99

14. JOHNNY CASH
00702615 Book/Online Audio $15.99

15. COUNTRY CLASSICS
00702834 Book/CD Pack $12.99

16. STANDARDS
00702835 Book/CD Pack $12.99

17. POP STANDARDS
00702836 Book/CD Pack $12.99

18. IRISH SONGS
00703086 Book/Online Audio $12.99

19. BLUES STANDARDS
00703087 Book/CD Pack $12.99

20. FOLK POP ROCK
00703088 Book/CD Pack $12.99

21. HAWAIIAN CLASSICS
00703097 Book/CD Pack $12.99

22. ISLAND SONGS
00703098 Book/CD Pack $12.99

23. TAYLOR SWIFT
00221966 Book/Online Audio $16.99

24. WINTER WONDERLAND
00101871 Book/CD Pack $12.99

25. GREEN DAY
00110398 Book/CD Pack $14.99

26. BOB MARLEY
00110399 Book/Online Audio $14.99

27. TIN PAN ALLEY
00116358 Book/CD Pack $12.99

28. STEVIE WONDER
00116736 Book/CD Pack $14.99

29. OVER THE RAINBOW & OTHER FAVORITES
00117076 Book/Online Audio $15.99

30. ACOUSTIC SONGS
00122336 Book/CD Pack $14.99

31. JASON MRAZ
00124166 Book/CD Pack $14.99

32. TOP DOWNLOADS
00127507 Book/CD Pack $14.99

33. CLASSICAL THEMES
00127892 Book/Online Audio $14.99

34. CHRISTMAS HITS
00128602 Book/CD Pack $14.99

35. SONGS FOR BEGINNERS
00129009 Book/Online Audio $14.99

36. ELVIS PRESLEY HAWAII
00138199 Book/Online Audio $14.99

37. LATIN
00141191 Book/Online Audio $14.99

38. JAZZ
00141192 Book/Online Audio $14.99

39. GYPSY JAZZ
00146559 Book/Online Audio $15.99

40. TODAY'S HITS
00160845 Book/Online Audio $14.99

HAL•LEONARD®

www.halleonard.com

1021
483

Prices, contents, and availability subject to change without notice.